For Laurie
Enjoy. Jerry

Up the Creek
Without a Saddle

The Bareback Poetry
of
Jerry Johnson

Jerry Johnson

Up the Creek Without a Saddle
Noah's Song

....

Order these books (**with FREE CDs**) for yourself, family
or friends on the author's website www.vtpoet.com.
Noah's Song and **Up the Creek Without a Saddle**
make for great gifts!

....

Website: www.vtpoet.com
Email: Jerry@vtpoet.com

Up the Creek Without a Saddle

The Bareback Poetry
of
Jerry Johnson

Creek Road Press

Irasburg, VT

in collaboration with

Virgo eBooks Publishing

Vergennes, VT

Published by Creek Road Press
PO Box 44, Irasburg, VT 05845 USA
www.vtpoet.com

in collaboration with

Virgo eBooks Publishing
4800 Basin Harbor Road, Vergennes, VT 05491 USA
www.virgoebooks.com

ISBN Paperback: 978-0-9897048-3-0
ISBN eBook: 978-0-9897048-6-1

Illustrations by Jerry Johnson

Book & Cover Design by Jerry Johnson

Dedication

In memory of my parents, Russell and Dagny,
who truly loved the Green Mountain State

Contents

Chapter 1: Gifts from Animals

Chapter 2: Natural Things

Chapter 3: The Human Element

Chapter 4: Time and Place

Kudos to Jerry's Poetry

"Reading Jerry's work sometimes feels to me like taking a brisk walk on a Vermont autumn day, with its crisp gusts of wind, changes of weather and mood, solemn moments and cheerful moments, tremendous energy, and the pleasure of sudden glimpses of lovely, unexpected light."
    —Reeve Lindbergh, celebrated author of adult and children's books

"Each poem in *Up the Creek Without a Saddle* is a celebration, and the addition of Pete's and Jon's musical renditions adds a rare 4th dimension."
    —Geof Hewitt, Vermont Poetry Slam Champion

"Good poetry is music in itself—any lover of words knows that. But it's not often that a book of poetry comes with a CD of music. That's the case with Northeast Kingdom Poet Jerry Johnson's new collection. The book, *Up the Creek Without a Saddle*, comes with a CD that features sixteen of his poems set to music written by Vermont musicians Jon Gailmor and Pete Sutherland. ... It's a dream come true for you, Jerry, and certainly a treat for us to read."
    —from Jerry's interview with Peter Biello on Vermont Public Radio

"These poems employ a host of techniques to bring us into a wonderful world: rhymes, rhythms, half-rhymes, unexpected images, familiar and unexpected turnings. Like the best lyrical poetry of all ages, the poems locate our hearts in a particular place. In this case, it's rural Vermont with all its beauty, hard-work, joys and sorrows. Set to the music of Jon Gailmor and Pete Sutherland, the poems in *Up the Creek Without a Saddle* are at once fresh, inviting, heart-felt and familiar. They resonate with real life."
    —Ray Hudson, author of *Moments Rightly Placed: An Aleutian Memoir*

"Jerry's poems resonate with a crystalline clarity and conviction, a true paean to rural Vermont."
    —Lynda Graham-Barber, author of *KokoCat - Inside and Out*

Preface

I live in the bucolic Northeast Kingdom of Vermont and feel fortunate to call this beautiful section of the Green Mountain State my home. In 1970, my father purchased a 76-acre farm in the Kingdom, complete with barn, farmhouse, fields, woods and streams. When he passed away in 1998, he left me the farm. It was an incredible gift.

For me, the farm has been heaven on earth. There is lots of room to hike with my dogs. Deer and other critters roam the property. Lord's Creek meanders through the meadows and is home to many brook trout. The farm has been a place to be creative, a place to inspire my interest in writing poetry.

The animals in my life have inspired much of my writing. I have had five horses living at my farm—a bay Morgan, an Appaloosa, a Quarter Horse mare, and her two fillies who were born at my homestead. I currently have two golden retrievers and an engaging barn cat.

A special bond exists between my animals and me. My horses brought life's positive energy to the farm. They gave this energy to the pasture, meadows, the barn and especially to people who visited. Each day I tried to teach them something. Each day they taught me something whether or not I was paying attention.

This book captures a bit of what I have learned from my four-legged friends both domesticated and wild. It also tries to describe the beauty and natural phenomena I have experienced.

I want my readers to share with me the autumn leaves, summer rains, antiquated stone walls snaking through the woods, maple sugaring in springtime, 30-below-zero winter days, the birth of a foal, mud season, apple blossoms surrounding my farm. In addition, I wanted to portray the personalities of a few unique people I have met in the Kingdom.

A dream of mine was fulfilled when Jon Gailmor and Pete Sutherland, two of Vermont's most beloved troubadours, took sixteen of my poems and set them to music. A CD of those songs is available on my website, www.vtpoet.com, and at Amazon as an audio CD.

May you have a pleasant journey through *Up the Creek Without a Saddle*.

Jerry Johnson

Bear Mountain Farm
East Albany, Vermont

Acknowledgements

It is with heartfelt gratitude that I thank the following poets and writers for their support, encouragement and savvy feedback: Howard Frank Mosher, Sydney Lea, Peggy Sapphire, Reeve Lindbergh, John Fusco, Geof Hewitt, Ray Hudson, Lynda Graham-Barber, Ron Lewis, Inga Potter, Matthew Mayo, Pat Goudey O'Brien and my editor Sue Roupp.

I thank digital photographer John Selmer for the outstanding job he did in turning my paintings into illustrations for this book.

I thank the following publications for providing me with venues to share my poems: *The Mountain Troubadour, The Poet's Touchstone, Caledonian Record, the Chronicle, Newport Daily Express, Vermont Poetry Newsletter, North Star Monthly, Green Mountain Trading Post, Hardwick Gazette, Vermont's Northland Journal* and *New England Senior Tennis Foundation Bulletin.*

I would also like to acknowledge the animals in my life who provided inspiration for many of my poems: My horses—Willoughby Skipper, Certified Cinda, Bear Mountain Creek and Cinda's Chocolate Peace —for keeping me honest with my feelings. My barn cats—Pinkie, Blackie and Lady Gray—whose antics made me into a cat lover. My golden retrievers—Vermont's Sundance and Sir Toby of Vermont— who have been my steadfast companions and enduring friends.

Special Thanks

I would like to give special thanks to Jon Gailmor and Pete Sutherland, two fine Vermont troubadours, for their wonderful musical renditions of a number of my poems. For each poem, I gave the artists free rein to come up with their own interpretations, complete with word changes and lyrical nuances, as they saw fit. Their songs held to the integrity of the poems while bringing them musical life. The final result is a delightful CD which is available on my website, www.vtpoet.com, and at Amazon as an audio CD.

Jon Gailmor: www.jongailmor.com
Pete Sutherland: www.epactmusic.com

Jerry's Poems Set to Music Album

Master musicians Jon Gailmor and Pete Sutherland sing and play the bareback poetry of Jerry Johnson. Sixteen selected poems from *Up the Creek Without a Saddle* are masterfully turned into an epic contemporary folk album, available on the poet's website www.vtpoet.com and at Amazon.com as an audio CD.

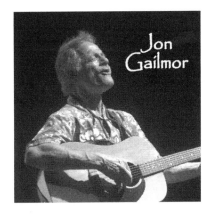

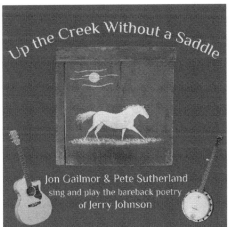

iPad and Mac users can download the premium interactive edition of *Up the Creek Without a Saddle* from iBookstore, containing both Jerry's poetry and the 16 songs from the music album.

Chapter 1

Gifts from Animals

Morgan horse painted on antique sap bucket cover

Gifts

The animals bring gifts—
howl of the wolf,
song of the songbird,
sonar boom of the humpback,
horse whinny of the untamed equus.

These roamers of plains,
nesters of forest,
deep water divers,
traversers of valley and hill,
living off instinct
as prey, as predators,
in balance,
taking what is vital,
returning the same.

These special creatures,
higher beings,
are living symbols of what we once were,
can again become

if, in silence,
we watch
and listen.

Nature's Beatitudes

Blessed is the barn swallow flying above,
blessed is the cooing of the mourning dove.

Blessed is the doe with her spotted fawn,
blessed are the sunset and the first light of dawn.

Blessed are the fishes and humpbacks of the sea,
blessed are the salmon and the native brookie.

Blessed are the hawk and the soaring eagle,
blessed are the kestrel and the cardinal so regal.

Blessed are the Mustang, the Morgan, the Paint,
and Francis of Assisi—all creatures' patron saint.

Blessed are Monarchs adrift in the sky
and Tiger Swallowtails so easy on the eye.

Blessed is the lion, blessed is the lamb,
blessed are the moose and the mountain ram.

Blessed are those who comprehend
all creatures are their brethren.
Blessed are the meek and merciful
for they shall find their heaven.

Resurrection

New foal,
you come into this world
with the sapience of your
ancestral brothers and sisters,
your equine imprint
fully formed at birth
as you suckle at your mother's side.

You feel the human's touch
as he lays hands
on your body, nurturing
an enduring bond.

In time,
in your own way,
you may teach the human
your primordial wisdom.

Blessed is the Broodmare

Blessed is the broodmare carrying her foal within,
Eleven months of patient waiting for her next of kin.
Fully without warning a filly does arrive
And sleeps on welcome bed of straw, so peacefully alive.

Blessed is the filly bringing calmness to the farm,
She senses that the horseman won't bring her any harm.
He kneels beside her body, strokes her face and mane,
The broodmare stands contented, no reason to complain.

On wobbly legs she suckles at her mother's teat,
The bond twixt mare and brand new foal is something truly sweet.
The broodmare's utmost purpose is to help her baby grow,
And teaching every little thing a horse will need to know.

Blessed is the broodmare bringing wonder to this earth
And hope to all of humankind with this wondrous birth.
There's nothing near as moving as a foal with cherished mare,
A broodmare and her filly—now that's a handsome pair.

Whispering Sweet Nothings

As I whisper sweet nothings to my horse
he never listens to me, of course.
It seems no matter what I do or say
his only interest is hay.

I try to impart the lessons of Lyons
but my steed just isn't trying.
When I attempt the works of Parelli
my colt just wants food in his belly.

Next time I'll apply the wisdom of Reis
to see, at last, if we find some peace.
Reis always essays what is natural,
his lessons appear quite rational.

I'll then employ Clint from down under
and hope for success, but I wonder.
Will my pony listen to me today
or will his mind still be on hay?

Dedicated to those impressive horse trainers — John Lyons, Pat Parelli,
Dennis Reis and Australian Clinton Anderson.

Eventide at the Pond

Hey, mister heron,
don't fly off ...
I'm trying to take your picture.

I look forward each evening
to watching you tippytoe in the shallow water
along the edges of the pond.
My only hope is that you leave
the brookies and rainbows alone.

If you're going to *fish,*
fish for crawdads which roam around the rocks.
They're such easy prey.

You're a majestic bird,
perhaps a descendant of the Pterodactyl
of the Jurassic era,
your body approaching five feet long,
wingspan of nearly eight.
They don't call you Great for nothing.

So, my dear heron,
I bid you adieu until tomorrow at eventide
when you will return to my pondside,

stand stock-still
like a statue (as herons are inclined to do),
patiently await a meal at twilight,

and pause a while
as I scramble for my camera
to capture you once again.

There's Nothing Like a Golden

There's nothing like a Golden
with their built-in smiles,
always glad to see you,
walk with you for miles.

And when the evening comes
they'll lay right at your feet.
Goldens are my choice of dog,
they're always truly sweet.

Merganser at My Pond

Hey Common Merganser
you're not that common to me

When you frequent my pond
it fills my heart with glee

Your feathers are exquisite
you are an Olympic swimmer

Come again in the moonlight
when your plumage will shimmer.

A Foal on its Second Day

Mother, mother, please come to me,
I need a nourishing drink from you.
I want to grow up big and strong;
right now I'm small, the world is new.

I'm not afraid, you're at my side
as I lie in a pasture of green.
You're the best mom a foal could have,
you'll protect me from things unseen.

Some day when I am trained and smart,
I'll win a blue ribbon at the fair.
But, for the moment I like it here,
I'm in good hands, without a care.

Horse Dances

Horses dance in a pasture,
vying for position in the herd,
each showing off its best moves,
heads held high, tails raised,
sashaying with each lifted hoof
arched like the arm of a conductor
holding a baton.

They race away across the meadow
and back again.
One assumes the forerunner's advantage
and then another.
The young foal keeps up,
her instinct not to lead but to join.

A protective, maternal mare
assumes the dominant position,
the role of alpha leader, of matriarch.
All ears turn to her silent, subtle commands,
heads are lowered in her presence.

A sequential order is laid down
from high to low,
each horse knowing
its standing in the herd.
A peaceful coexistence is set in a pasture
among the dancing horses.

Ballet

Have you ever heard the hoof
poundings of a steed as he glides
along the firm earth below?

Watch and you will see Vaslav Nijinsky
as he prances and leaps through the pasture

Soon he is joined by Anna Pavlova
prima ballerina of the meadow
They dance as one
Their rhythmic juxtaposition of hoof falls
is a tantalizing drumbeat
as they canter side by side

A ballet they perform
Romeo and Juliet
followed by *Don Quixote*
Watch closely as they sprint
soar and spin
all in perfect syncopation

Close your eyes and listen
for they may not pass this way again
and you will have missed
the Imperial Ballet de Caballos.

Peaceful Luckiness

Luck is a result of good planning,
so I guess it was not mere chance
to have produced my Chocolate Peace,
such a pretty foal at a glance.

Lots of work and wise preparation
were needed if she was to be;
it is such a treat to pet her,
her head resting soft on my knee.

Nothing happens just by accident,
success comes if you pay the price.
On the long road to reaching your goals,
it's not a matter of rolling dice.

Whether or not you reach your dreams,
vision and effort mustn't cease.
Perhaps if you give it your all,
you, too, will find your Peace.

Cinda's
Chocolate Peace

Spring Fever

A horse on the run
In the noonday sun
Is thinking of you today.
She hopes you're as blissful and joyful as she,
She'd want it no other way.

Run, my filly, run!
Sprint like the wind!
Let your mane and tail ripple with their wild, majestic magic.
Run, my filly, run!

Jump! Leap!
Let your hoof-falls boom across the meadow,
Pulsate on distant hills.

Caress the air,
Stroke the earth,
As you tie them together on your springtime romp.

Run, my filly, run!
Kick up your heels!
While the stars and moon in the night sky applaud your every move,
Run, my filly, run!

A horse on the run
In the noonday sun
Is thinking of you today.
She hopes you're as blissful and joyful as she,
She'd want it no other way.

A Woman and Her Horse

Two friends take a walk down a gentle lane.
She guides with a gentle touch,
the lead rope held loosely in her hand,
hanging freely from his halter.
A special, unspoken bond exists
between the woman and her horse.
No words are needed to express their oneness.

A gentle breeze blows through trees and fields
which border their path,
causing her hair and his mane to sway
from side to side.

Each reflects on the moment and nothing more.
Her mind is freed up from
the everyday happenings of a busy life.
His mind has never been caught up with such things.

They walk for miles and know
that each is a mentor to the other.
It brings her contentment.
It brings him freedom.
And it brings both to the realization
that they are inseparable.

A Bed of Clover

Beneath a bed of clover
  below the melting snow,
  the thundering hoof beats
  of wild horses resound,
    liberated from encumbrances,
    unbound from harness and halter,
    free from fenced-in pasture.
  An ethereal presence is felt,
  roaming and galloping
  through meadow and wood
beneath a bed of clover.

Beneath a bed of leaves
  decaying layer on layer,
  lie remnants of the past,
    a maze of earthen smells forgotten,
    horses with whom
      our bonds have diverged,
  trails we took and didn't take,
  all decaying layer on layer
beneath a bed of leaves.

Beneath a bed of hay
  memories slip away to dust
    of horsemen who came and went,
    of creatures of the wild,
    of sights and sounds
    of whinnying friends.
  All sought to offer balance,
  they now lie fast asleep
beneath a bed of hay.

Beneath a bed of grass
   each blade gives up its life,
   yet gives life.
      Tiny oaks begin their push
        to reach morning light,
      crickets chirp,
      lilies free their bonds,
      mares give birth to foals.
   The compost of our past transgressions
   forms fodder for new life.
   Our roots spread deeper as we draw
   rekindled strength
beneath a bed of grass.

Upon a bed of clover
   all things old are born anew,
      as fillies and colts, without a blemish,
      ascend to the sun
      to start once more with shackles gone,
      to stretch and touch their dreams.
   A new beginning comes,
   with forgiveness and rebirth,
   rooted deep and pressing out
upon a bed of clover.

Beneath a bed of clover,
   beneath a bed of leaves,
      beneath a bed of hay,
   beneath a bed of grass,
upon a bed of clover.

For Pete's Sake

for Pete the Moose

There's a moose whose home is in Irasburg,
Many folks are concerned for his life.
As he roams behind fenced-in quarters,
He is happy and should never face strife.

David Lawrence and Pete are good buddies,
It's a special bond between man and beast.
David is Pete's Saint Francis of Assisi
Here in the Kingdom Northeast.

Pete the Moose has gained attention
From near and from faraway.
While most folks are rooting for Pete's life,
There are a few who think he must pay ...

Pay with his life, they put forward,
A moose with elk shouldn't be roaming.
Shoot Pete the Moose with a gun
And ship all the elk back to Wyoming.

Now, it is time to leave Pete alone,
Where he's safe and should live out his life.
As he roams behind fenced-in quarters,
He is happy and should never face strife.

Noah's Song

Have you ever seen llamas wearing pajamas
or a dancing cow in a herd?
Or a big bull moose atop a caboose?
Are all my questions absurd?

I was building an ark when I heard my dog bark
at a long-haired orangutan.
The sight of this ape with a muscular shape
was enough to frighten any man.

Just the other day while out making hay
I saw a vision that made me take heed—
A black and white skunk dressed like a monk,
riding a unicorn steed.

Then I spotted a cheetah eating Velveeta,
playing chess with a colorful bird.
The bird, though colossal, seemed quite docile,
I hope you're not doubting my word.

    Amphibians, reptiles, mammals
    Come aboard without a fear
    From a horned toad to a lumpy camel
    Different as can be, but all family
    On the Ark—survival is the name of the game
    On the Ark—doesn't matter from whence you came
    On the Ark we're all equal, all the same
    On the Ark.

I spied an old goat rowing a boat
crammed with cats and dogs,
along with a lion, chopping onions and cryin'
to the music of a pond full of frogs.

Up in the sky elephants did fly
with the ease of eagles on wing.
Alas, an alpaca ran right smacka
into a panda going to Beijing.

A goose and a rabbit developed a habit
of scaring a giraffe and a yak.
But they'd run off in fright at the hideous sight
fending off their sneaky attack.

A smiling green dragon was pulling a wagon
loaded with chickens and sheep.
It was such a weird vision, they had a collision
with some ducks who were trying to sleep.

 Amphibians, reptiles, mammals
 Come aboard without a fear
 From a horned toad to a lumpy camel
 Different as can be, but all family
 On the Ark—survival is the name of the game
 On the Ark—doesn't matter from whence you came
 On the Ark we're all equal, all the same
 On the Ark.

I was filled with remorse till I spotted a horse
who jumped through a big ring of fire.
A donkey was cheering as the horse started rearing
at a worm in the muck and the mire.

A hippie hippopotamus drove a big yellow bus
of critters on their way to school.
Each funny creature had an apple for the teacher
except for the obstinate mule.

I next heard a laugh from a gangly giraffe
in pursuit of a speedy gazelle.
The gazelle had her tricks and avoided the kicks
of the giraffe who started to yell.

It was surely a jinx when I noticed a lynx
sneaking through the woods at my farm.
And it was clearly preposterous to spy a rhinoceros
giving me cause for alarm.

    Amphibians, reptiles, mammals
    Come aboard without a fear
    From a horned toad to a lumpy camel
    Different as can be, but all family
    On the Ark—survival is the name of the game
    On the Ark—doesn't matter from whence you came
    On the Ark we're all equal, all the same
    On the Ark.

Armored like a gladiator came an angry alligator
making my spine start to shiver.
But 'twas a crocodile with his toothy big smile
which caused my whole body to quiver.

A catamount crawling on his belly and a'bawling
made the hair on my head stand straight.
However, seeing a mouse on the floor of my house
was the one thing I surely did hate.

Soon all the beasts filled the ark I did build,
a zooful on every floor.
I stood there confounded, totally astounded,
a spectacle too hard to ignore.

Heed the words I've spoken, keep your eyes wide open
to the creatures in the air and on ground.
You'll never know when you'll see them again
or some others just as profound.

    Amphibians, reptiles, mammals
    Come aboard without a fear
    From a horned toad to a lumpy camel
    Different as can be, but all family
    On the Ark—survival is the name of the game
    On the Ark—doesn't matter from whence you came
    On the Ark we're all equal, all the same
    On the Ark.

Ralph the Rooster and Henrietta the Hen

There once was a radiant rooster
Who fell for a radiant hen.
They lived together in harmony
And hugged every now and then.

Henrietta never henpecked her lover
And Ralph let her cluck-cluck all day.
They would frolic in the barnyard
And cavort in the new mown hay.

At sunrise he would cock-a-doodle-do
And she would come a'running.
Henrietta was crazy about her Ralph
And she also looked quite stunning.

People came from miles around
To see Ralph and Henrietta.
The two would sing in the barnyard
Just like in an operetta.

Yes, a rooster and hen can be buddies
And have fun in the summer sun,
And sleep on a roost side-by-side
Whenever the day is done.

Little Bundles

Little bundles of energy
With motors running fast
Not a mouse stands a chance
Their fates are surely cast

Cats can sleep for hours
Upon a bed of hay
Yet never miss a trick
Throughout the night and day

They're sentries of their fort
Will hide when you walk by
Love it when you bring food
Cats are smart and sly

Little bundles of energy
Rascals around the clock
They do everything impromptu
Their schedules are ad hoc.

Best Friend

Each day   at least once a day
I look him in the eye
and say *Thank you for being here*
He seems to understand
as he lies there   head resting
on his front paws   eyeing me
raising one brow
and then the other

He gives me a certain attentive look
whenever I speak   It appears
that he takes in every word
Sometimes I say *Cookie*
which causes him to spring to his feet
There's something doggy magical
about the word *cookie*

Walk is another word
which promptly gets his attention
perhaps even more than *cookie*
He flies to the door
body all aquiver
waiting for me to take him for a stroll
His face says *Speed it up! Let's go!*

Each night
I say *Thank you for being here*
as he slumbers by the side of my bed
dreaming of cookies and walks.

My Morgan

At dawn my young bay Morgan
stands poised like a regal statue
on the crest of a knoll
head held high
neck curved like the arc of a quarter moon
winter coat of thickened hair
buffering the chill of daybreak
Willoughby Skipper is a chiseled silhouette
of a proud breed

A thin wire strung
from cedar post to cedar post
keeps him from the freedom once enjoyed
by his founding ancestor
more than two hundred years ago
Justin Morgan's diminutive stallion *Figure*
begetter of legends

My Skipper stands in worthy testament
to his proud lineage
and sees beyond the threadlike line
to the beckoning meadow and woods
He watches me leave the barn
a bale of hay in each hand for balance
as I walk to the pasture

He gallops with the ease of a dancer to greet me
bits of snow flinging from his feet
each cadenced hoof-fall
resounding off the frozen earth
ringing through our valley
and its attendant hills

His conformation is perfect
his musculature is powerful
from shoulder to hindquarter
I lay the hay atop the drifting snow
Skipper gently whinnies
We pause in silence   man and horse
I ponder   *Do I have dominion over him?*
I think not

I have taken him into my world
He has allowed me into his
He succumbs to my requests
as I whisper my instructions
We share in Communion
He seems to know what I am thinking
even if I do not whisper
I measure him in hands
He stands still and noble on hooves of steel
measuring me

I open the gate
and turn to say *Skipper let's go*
But he is already there
just behind my right shoulder
No need for bridle and lead rope

I brush his body's chestnut coat
from withers to croup
remove briars from his mane
He nudges me tenderly on the arm
as my currycomb massages chest and girth

My gift to him is to provide the food and shelter
that his ancestors sought in the wild
Skipper's gift is the permission he grants me
to be part of his world
There is divinity
in his equanimity.

You Are the Horse

You are the horse—
dancer, prancer,
leaper and turner

mystical Morgan
who rises and falls in
effortless magic,

hooves digging deep
into the yielding earth
of a forest floor or verdant meadow.

In the wild,
even among those who breathe the breaths
of the two-legged,

they pause to watch the horse
sashay his way
into their souls.

Old Friend

Old horse   old friend
your mane of flaxen hair still shines
when the early morning sun hits it right

Stay yet another day
for me to do my chores
Let me fetch you a bale of fresh hay
and fill your pail with clear water
one more time
Let me stroke your aging body
with my wrinkled hand

Grand times in days gone by
together we did ride
saddle draped behind your sturdy shoulders
You held me safe and high   you knew my every thought
as your fluid movement matched the grace
of a Baryshnikov

You pulled the sleigh along forest paths
and high-stepped through white meadows
as winter bells rang out our presence
On summer days
in harness to a buggy
we ventured down country lanes
The humming of the old-style wooden wheels
and the rhythmic beat of your four hooves
clip clop clippity clop   *clip clip clippity clop*
on the gravel road still reverberate in my mind

Stay yet another day
and let me give you grain
for time is near when you will pass
and time for me to shed a tear
We are one   the two of us
so let me brush your coat
clean your stall
and lay down fresh wood shavings

Old friend   dear old friend
cherished pal for life
companion of mine forever
my soulmate sublime

Stay yet another day
so we can saddle up
One more ride across the muted meadow
I'll hitch you to that sleigh
We'll travel down a gentle lane
again bells peal and we dream of times
when we were one and young

Your mane of flaxen hair still shines
when the early morning sun hits it right
So stay yet one more day
old horse   old friend.

Last Horse Out of the Barn

The last one left today
trailered away behind a pickup truck
Each of my horses has found a new home
My barn is empty   so am I

Tears readily fall from my eyes
even as I write this testament
and I wonder if horses cry

Will they remember me
Will they forgive me
Do they know my decision was from the heart
Will they stay connected with me
communicate with me though miles separate us
Do they know that my soul
will always stay bonded to them
Or did they take my soul with them

Do they know that they were my healers
my confidants
Will they miss seeing me each morning
bringing them hay
some grain   an apple   a carrot

Will they stand by a fence at their new homes
and wonder if I will be bringing them
their evening bale of sweet hay
Will they have visions of me
dressed in coveralls

approaching with treats in my pocket
Will they yearn for my touch   my voice
Will they miss having me groom them
with a currycomb and brush

I think about them everyday
They have left a mystical mark
Their spirits still reside at the farm
I still hear soothing nickers
in the barren windswept pasture
Whinnies pulsate off the boards of each stall

I still smell the sweet aroma of the horse
the perfume of Pegasus   that earthy smell
emanating from sculptured robust bodies
I still hear the rhythmic hoof-poundings
of galloping horses
ricocheting off Chamberlin Hill

I thank each of my horses
for their journey with me upon this earth
They gave me ways of healing
and filled my life with mirth
May we still ride the trail together
although we are apart
I'll ne'er forget my horses
They will stay within my heart.

Chapter 2

Natural Things

Pen and ink drawing of a Northeast Kingdom brook trout

Hidden Place

for my mother

There is a hidden place
   in the cedar woods
   just above the creek.

A grand old willow across the flowing water
   and three giant pines
     along Creek Road
are the only ones
that can see this place.

The willow's drooping thin arms quiver
   as it gazes
   and tries reaching to this place.
The tall conifers' numerous cones,
   beaconing lighthouse eyes,
     tearfully blink
as they peruse this hidden place …

this place with a stool of stone and root,
   woven together by the fabric
   of life and dreams,
   a seat for you, alone.
This place and seat were placed there
out of inspiration for your purpose,
   alone.

Seat yourself.
Tune in to the smells,
    sounds, sights
        that come and go.
And gently gaze back
    to the willow to calm
    its thin arms,
        and to the three pines
to dry their soulful eyes.

Summer Cloudburst

From out of nowhere
    they slowly build
        thickening thunderheads
        of the cumulonimbus
     gathering force
     to rewrite the story
of this clear summer sky

With the might of a philharmonic
    the heavens are swept
    with a symphonic jousting of
        clashing cornets
        mournful cellos
        doleful oboes
boastful bass drums

With curtains drawn
    ragged bolts of blazing light
        whipcrack across the pressing sky
        flaying open a summer cloudburst
        to spread baptismal waters
    to purify the land
    and cleanse the souls
of those who are too grounded.

I love trees and more than likely I will never see (or write) a poem as lovely as one. While driving on a back road here in Vermont, I came across one of the most incredible trees I have ever seen anywhere in New England. I had to stop and check it out. It was a sugar maple of such size and grandeur that I could hardly believe my eyes.

Luckily I had my camera and 100-foot tape measure with me and proceeded to take pictures and measurements. The tree's diameter near its base was 6 feet and its trunk's circumference ranged between 18 and 19 feet. With the application of a bit of algebra, I determined the tree's height to be around 100 feet. My biggest question was how old it was. I knew it was more than 200 years old. I knew it had lived through many historical events that have occurred in Vermont, the rest of the country and the world. I had a good feeling that it was around when the Green Mountain Boys were roaming the hills.

I did some research and found a formula to roughly estimate the age of this stately maple. I entered appropriate numbers into the formula and determined that the maple's age was somewhere between 330 and 360 years. That meant that this particular Acer saccharum was a baby tree somewhere between 1650 and 1680. The Pilgrims landed on Plymouth Rock in 1620. Vermont joined the federal Union in 1791 as the fourteenth state, becoming the first state to enter the Union after the original thirteen colonies. Perhaps some of the Green Mountain Boys had climbed this tree. This proud sugar maple had assuredly lived through and witnessed a lot of history.

I was sure that this maple had a few stories buried under its thick layer of bark and I wondered if I could coax a story or two out of it and write a poem. Here is my attempt to pay homage to this beautiful sugar maple which took three centuries to reach its majestic stature.

The Witness

O, majestic sugar maple,
what have you seen throughout your lifetime?
You have lived through fifteen score or more years
here in the Kingdom where rivers flow north.
Immobile you stand on your footing,
your monolithic roots run haphazardly in all directions,
your gigantic branches stretch upward to the heavens—
a witness you have been to a world going by.

What have you been privy to?
Are your secrets hidden just beneath
the surface of your thick, gnarly bark,
or are they buried deep inside,
bonded to each of your growth rings?

Perhaps …
    a million tears have been shed
    under your branches
    and your comforting canopy of green
    has dried those tears.

Perhaps …
    you held a tree house in your limbs,
    kids in knickerbockers climbed all over you,
    a swing hung from a mammoth branch.

Perhaps …

>   shaded by your crown,
>   lovers made love on a blanket
>   and carved their initials into your bark.
>   Perhaps a young soldier and his bride
>   made their wedding vows under you.

Perhaps …

>   that young soldier was a Green Mountain Boy
>   who lost his life in battle,
>   leaving his bride to weep under you.

Perhaps …

>   you provided cover for deer and catamounts,
>   shade for cows and horses,
>   a home for a robin or bluebird,
>   a refuge for an eagle or hawk.

Perhaps …

>   you survived a bolt of lightning,
>   a hurricane or tempestuous twister,
>   the weight of a snow-dumping winter storm,
>   a time of drought.

Perhaps …
      a young lady lay on one of your huge limbs
      as she read *Little Women*.
      A young poet positioned himself
      into a crooked crotch
      and penned his first poem
      and read it aloud to milady.

O, august sugar maple,
you have so many tales buried beneath
that thick layer of bark.
Might I tap into you during the sugaring season
to let your stories flow freely
into my story-gathering bucket?

Perhaps, just perhaps, a poem will percolate
through the layers of my mind
to be penned on paper—
a poem I can share with others …

And then, O dear maple,
you will rest in peace when your time comes,
assured and content that your story was told.

Survival

Autumn departed long ago
and with it she took
her russet leaves
fresh scented days
soft evening breeze

Valley dew has turned into rime
Distant hills are laden with
skeletons of barren trees

Birds hunger for filled feeders
Bucks maneuver
rut   strut   draw lots
to claim their does

Vermont will claim its survivors
those who will stick it out
rough it out
as winter wails its warnings
in snow   wind   ice
and tumbling temperatures.

Thirty Below

People may say I'm from Vermont,
a handsome state, summer and fall;
even spring is a blessing
although through the mud we must crawl.

Winter in the Northeast Kingdom
is only for the brave of heart;
as temperatures plunge below zero,
many flatlanders depart.

With several layers on my body,
I constantly stoke the fire.
I look through my frosted-up window—
snow's getting higher and higher.

Yes, Vermont is a beautiful state
and to that everyone agrees,
but lately it's feeling like *Brrrr-mont*
from my head clear down to my knees.

Snow

The snow's a-coming
No ifs, ands, or buts
I think we should all
Stay in our huts

Eighteen-plus inches
Will fill up the drive
I don't know how
To put up with this jive

I should have stayed
All snug in my bed
As I peered through the window
And saw something to dread

I must feed the barn cats
I must feed the horses
I'll put on my jumpsuit
Though I'm filled with remorses

And head to the barn
Grab a couple of bales
Then march to the pasture
With snow up to our tails

My horses will whinny
And ask *Where have you been?*
We've been waiting for you
since we don't know when.

However the barn cats
Both Blackie and Gray
Will give the thumps up
As they cavort in the hay

Sunny and Toby
Will greet my return
As I enter the farmhouse
With my look of concern

They'll wag their tails
Give a golden grin
My dogs and I
Are next of kin

So here's my advice
On a day like today
Don't venture out
Or you will pay.

Apple Blossoms

One week or two each year,
the apple blossoms come,
from nature's varied palette,
a blaze of pink and plum.
Among the russet branches
of Braeburn and Pippin,
a blaze of red and yellow,
whose scents leave me smitten.

A broad canopy of peach,
a splash of white and gold,
is atop the wild Macouns,
quite awesome to behold.
The bold Baldwin soon joins in,
crimson all upon it,
and the Winesap, not outdone,
wears its Easter bonnet.

My antiquated grove
brings forth what it renders,
a kaleidoscopic blast
in its springtime splendors.
All the beauty that I see,
with its sacred powers,
brings me to creation's gate,
endures a mere few hours.

Sadly prematurely,
the pastel petals fall;
ghostly rains of muted hues
descend with nature's call.
Like gentle drops from heaven
they seek their resting tomb,
and I must wait another year
to see my wild trees bloom.

Hail to Cedar

Cedar is a magical wood
which weathers naturally as it should
A nice gray tone it will attain
and last forever in spite of rain

The incredible patterns and textures of cedar
are truly beautiful   nothing is neater
Honey colors which fade into grays
Hail to Cedar in so many ways.

Great Blue Heron

Great Blue Heron, at the edge of my pond,
your sorcerous neck is like a magic wand.

Alone you abide, frozen is your stance,
you seem mesmerized as if in a trance.

What are you seeking as you slowly traipse along?
Your beak is a weapon, an archer's mighty prong.

Is it crayfish you seek? An unsuspecting trout?
Perhaps a frog or two on your sneaky walkabout?

I, too, stand captivated—you have brightened up the day.
With your regal beauty, I hope that you will stay.

Quietly I linger and watch you do your thing,
it would be sad right now for you to take to wing.

Ensemble

A casual ensemble of leaves

rises up
and circles

in crazed delight
into a whirlwind

Their dance is my dance.

A Touch of Blue

When a bluebird appears
he does so as an ethereal apparition
arousing cerulean specters from his past

A splash of sapphire is he
blending all too well with the clear blue sky
Yet when he sings in your presence
you know you are the chosen one

If you are melancholy from
the issues of the day
his azure beauty and song of joy
will be the antidote to your sadness.

Rain I

Waking in the early morn
I hear the sound of rain
pummeling the metal roof
and pouring down the drain
I think I'll just lie awhile
and listen to the beat
of rhythmic syncopation
as drops and metal meet.

Season Change

Autumn has come
on the paws of a little bear
Dew in the valleys
turns into rime
Hills are afire
in orange and red
Geese in their V
fly to the south
Fawns in the wood
have lost their spots
Bucks are maneuvering
drawing lots

There's change in the air
a time to ponder
Soon Autumn will leave
over hills yonder.

When There's Moonlight in Vermont

This simple poem comes to you
from my barn along Lord's Creek
as I sit with all my horses
sharing tales which seem so meek

When there's moonlight in Vermont
the stars ascend above
symbols of redeeming hope
from the creator's love

There must have been a horse or two
in a stable faraway
and other creatures of this earth
close by where baby lay.

Rain II

Waking in the early morn
To the sound of rain
As it pummels on the metal roof
It's driving me insane
Enough I say   It has to stop
The grass has grown too tall
I cannot mow these blades of green
In this incessant squall
We need the sun   Where has it been?
It's time for it to shine
I get grumpier every day
And all I do is whine
I'll find a different chore to do
Something to light a spark
I think I'll grab some boards and nails
And start to build an ark.

Winter Snow

Winter snow in the Kingdom is where it's supposed to be,
Not in Virginia or the Carolinas where it's up to their knee.
The skiers in Vermont welcome trails with the stuff,
They love schussing down the slopes and carving through the fluff.

March is just around the corner, soon sugaring will commence,
The sugarman will start a'boiling and the sap will then condense.
Liquid gold from his arch will be bottled for the table,
Each container will be stamped with a *Grade A Light Amber* label.

One never knows when the snow will melt away,
When buds will start appearing and flowers bring forth bouquet.
I'll just have to sit here typing and compose a poem or two
And wait till the day we can say *Winter, adieu, adieu!*

Mud Season

It's mud season here in The Kingdom
my muffler is lost in the mire
my wheels are encrusted with muck
there's a *thump-thump-thump* in my tire

The undercarriage is in shambles
as it scrapes through all of this slop
I'm feeling dreadful and then
my humble jalopy does stop

I look for some help but where is it?
These roads are in need of a trim
I sit here and swear like a trooper
my situation's utterly grim

As I ponder the sad dilemma
of what has happened to my life
there appears a rescuing tow truck
I'm yanked from inglorious strife.

Norse God

What's with this weather?
Rain yesterday, rain the week before,

nothing but repetitive rain.
Pitiful, pathetic, prolonged rain.

What now? Hail? Give me a break.
Hailstones hammer my metal roof

with the palpitating pounding of
frigid, frozen chunks of ice.

In the heavens
Thor slams his heavy hammer,

sending off boastful blasts,
thundering bolts and bellicose bellows.

And the mighty oak bends,
bows and breaks.

Chapter 3

The Human Element

Sugar house painted on antique sap bucket cover

Sugaring

for Byron Cook, Vermont sugarman

Sugaring is his birthright,
passed down by his father and grandfather.
He has done it for sixty years.
It's a tradition, an annual springtime ritual
that courses through his veins
like the sap passing through the sapwood
of his sugarbush.

His leathered face furrows
like the bark of the maples he taps.
Each year the maples gain yet another ring;
each year his face earns another wrinkle.
It's tough work, transforming forty gallons
of watery sap into one gallon of syrup
for the table.

He works alone.
Sweat pours off his brow as sap boils.
The fire from the glowing arch
squirts shimmering lines of light
between the boards of his sugar house.
Each spring sap flows. Cold nights
and warm days make for good runs.

Writer's Block

It's one of those days I sometimes fear,
a day of writer's block.
There's a poem in me
but the words are not coming together.

So, I'll find some used bricks and chip away
at the decaying mortar still attached.
I'll grab a log-splitting axe
and dissever a few maple blocks
into firewood for next year's winter.

I'll let sweat pour freely from my brow.
My muscles and mind need such a workout.
The cobwebs will clear from my brain.
Thoughts will begin to flow.

Soon the words will arise.
I'll lay down the axe,
take a shower, grab a pen
and let the words spring forth.

Spontaneous Combustion

Excitement grows as the words
quickly fall into place—
each thought swiftly assembling
the right adjective, the ideal verb,
the perfect prepositional phrase.
Nothing gets in the way
as the poet senses Frost and Yeats
guiding his pen
which flows effortlessly
on a page in his notebook.

The phraseology is right on,
he has hit the mother lode.
The publishers will now come to him
and his career will then explode.

The Painter and the Poet

for John Pitcher, Vermont artist

One paints
finding it much easier
to brush on the changing shades
of a fallen shadow
than describe it in words

The other writes
painting pictures with words
trying to capture a scene or moment in his mind
trying to find the words
each word crucial
his final goal to move the reader
to recall a similar scene or moment

One keeps nature journals
recording the details so eventful at the time
Then he turns to sketching
when his verbal descriptions are insufficient
to describe what he will paint

The other keeps mental journals
storing away the particulars of things that matter
with the possibility that some day
a poem may arise

Each feels the other is blessed with a gift
one with a brush
the other with a pen
both trying to describe to others
an encounter that has enriched their lives

They are evangelists
called to preach the gospel
of the beautiful and precious
like a brownish
pink crested female cardinal
on a spring eve.

Upon Receiving Mary's Letter

for Mary Volkert

At ninety-three
her hand
is not as steady
as it was at nine
when she would run
through meadows
and stop now and then
to pick wild daisies.
While running and picking
she would hum
and sing
whatever came to her.
She could have cared less
if someone was listening.
But at ninety-three
she can write a poem
and tell of her days
of daisy picking
as she ran uninhibited
through meadows.
She is still humming
and singing,
finding a song and poem
in her heart
to share with you
and me.

Unencumbered Cucumbers

I've given up shopping in the traditional sense—
    writing down a list,
    finding loose cash on the counter
    and in various frayed pockets of well-worn Carhartts,
    driving thirty miles to Shaw's,
    pushing a cart up and down encumbered aisles—
doing all this for a chance to squeeze a melon
or the Charmin when no one's looking.
No, no more.

I'd rather grab a wicker basket and head out back
    to my garden to see what ripened overnight.
    My overly horse-manured plot
    grows vegetation like there is no tomorrow,
    sustains just about everything I've planted
and things I didn't.

My search begins among the weeds of my jungle.
    Ah, three ripe Early Girl tomatoes.
    I tenderly pick them.
    Now, where's the romaine lettuce?
    There she is, her leafy hands
    rising in morning prayer,
    pushing weeds aside.
I harvest a few tender leaves.

But there is more as my quest continues—
    red and green string beans,
    multi-headed, muscular broccoli
    and buried, sleepy carrots
soon find their way into my basket.

Maneuvering in fear of stepping on
a fresh veggie camouflaged by weeds,
    my feet feel something.
    Reaching down, my hand touches
    a blessed cuke
    and then another.
They, too, find their way into my basket.

What more could a guy want
    other than an early morning traipse
    through his garden,
    wearing comfortable coveralls,
    and uncovering
tasty tomatoes, luscious lettuce, brisk beans,
green-branched broccoli, crunchy carrots
and unencumbered cucumbers.

Throwing Out Stuff

Where did all this stuff come from?
Boxes filled with receipts and tax returns
dating back to the seventies.
Autographed photos of high school classmates,
letters from old girlfriends,
books, books, and more books ...

Christmas and birthday cards,
pictures of nieces and nephews,
tarnished silverware, dented pots and pans,
toasters, glasses, water-stained paintings,
dishes, dishes, and more dishes ...

Boxes laden with miscellaneous objects—
loose change, pencils, pens,
clothes pins, paper clips,
floppy disks, notepads.

It's time to rent a dumpster,
to clean house, to throw away
the haphazard assortment of collected belongings—
stuff that was at one point in time important,
stuff that I have possessed,
but over time has possessed me.
I will take my freedom back.

Oh, I may save the photo
of the comely blond tennis player
and the letter she sent.
I may save a tennis trophy or two
and cling to a few things of the past.

Alas, it's time to move on,
to clear the rubble of the past,
to toss it away.

All that is important I will carry within me
and write about it in a poem or two.

No Good Deed

You go out on a limb because
you always have
to help someone you feel
needs or wants some help

You sense they've had a tough time
or perhaps even a tough life

You have always trusted too much
and it makes no difference if
the person is a man or woman
a boy or girl
Age and gender are never factors
in your wanting to help

It's not because you seek
something in return
Most are truly appreciative of
your freely given support
and express words of gratitude

Some simply smile
Some say thank you
Some say nothing but their
faces say it all
And that is quite sufficient

For reasons not understood
some blame you and others
for their failures
for their inadequacies
their places in life

Some readily accept your gestures
of goodwill
then throw daggers
into your back

Some live like leeches
parasites
bloodsuckers

They know the system
and easily take from it
manipulate it

They have perfected their
own little systems
their modes of operation

They know there are those
who are readily sympathetic
They have no qualms
in taking advantage of another's benevolence

Will you ever learn
not to trust?
Will you continue to render support
to those you perceive as needy?

When will you learn that
no good deed goes unpunished?

When will you know
it is best not to help
that it is best to simply let them
wallow away with the wicked?

Moving On

You and your partner have parted ways
with not a chance for a friendship to endure

From what you have told me
and from what I have heard
she was not the woman for you
not a woman of ethics or moral fiber

I heard she shacked up with other men
even in your own home
I heard she would not only tell white lies
but lies more colorful than a rainbow

Her goal was to bring you to your knees
to emasculate you   to render you helpless

She tried to take away your essence
your heart   soul   mind
your very masculinity
and leave you with nothing

She thrived on your generosity
your good spirit
but nothing could satiate the savage beast
A toxic vampire was she
who wanted to impale the jugular

She wanted you curled up
in a fetal position   with no heartbeat
no breath   nothing

You made the right decision to move on
Let her wallow away
with the wicked

Her time may come
It is not for you to decide
The cosmos will do its thing

It was a rough journey for you
but you are the better for it
Your veracity has endured

The cosmos recognizes
your core is strong
You will continue
to maintain your generous spirit

Those with upright principles
those with honest intents
will gravitate to you

You are resilient and have grown
yet still the gentle soul
you have always been

Invado pacis
Go in peace.

It's a Difficult Age

It's a difficult age when you are one year old
You really don't know how to speak
in order to ask for something
More than likely you can barely walk

It's a difficult age when you are five years old
You are forced out of the house
away from your mommy to attend kindergarten

It's a difficult age when you turn twelve
You almost wish you could skip twelve and be thirteen
You yearn to be a teenager
You're concerned about how your hair looks
You have a crush on a thirteen year old girl
who will not talk to you because of the age difference

It's a difficult age being fifteen
You wonder if you're popular
You like older girls
You wonder if you can get a date
You want to drive but have no license
You waste Saturdays and Sundays sleeping until noon

It's a difficult age being twenty
almost a man
You're looking for the right woman
You're in college hoping to graduate
hoping to get a good job
You yearn to be twenty-one

It's a difficult age hitting thirty
They call it The Big 3-0
Holy Mackerel   this is serious
Have you grown up?
Have you figured out what to do with your life?
When will you settle down?

It's a difficult age when you hit forty
You like younger women
You're concerned about your hair   what's left of it
You're wearing glasses to see the computer screen
You can barely fit into your jeans
without holding in your gut

It's a difficult age when fifty, sixty and seventy arrive
Wait a minute
what happened to those three decades?
You can't find your glasses
Your jeans do not fit anymore
You can't touch your toes
You read the obituaries everyday
and are thankful your name isn't there
You still like younger women

It's a difficult age when you are eighty
You have trouble speaking
in order to ask for something
More than likely you can barely walk
You yearn for the good old days
when you were totally confident
and the chicks really dug you.

My Niece, The Thinker

It's me Karin   the thinker am I
I ponder deeply about the sun and sky
I answer questions only after much thought
Give me some time if it's wisdom being sought

I contemplate the heavens   freedom of speech
Encourage my students whenever I teach
Each word in a poem or story I write
Must be filled with the deepest insight

Marriage   babies   the herstory of the world
Be patient and sapience will be unfurled
My drummer beats to the cosmos   you see
Be patient I say   and you'll hear my decree

My guitar and I   we put words into song
I hope those who listen will know they belong
Keith by my side joins Katie and Beth
A quartet of singers to take away your breath

Yes it's me Karin   the thinker I am
I am tough as a lion yet meek as a lamb
And what you will get from the words I impart
Lightning from the heavens going to your heart.

Ride 'em, Pecos Bill

for my friend who has a tough time staying in the saddle

Listen my children and you will hear
Of the midday ride of Bill, so dear.
He was thrown from Abby one more time,
Again ending up on his cushiony behind.

No helmet upon his head does he wear—
It's as if he doesn't really care.
The advice from his trainers he will not take.
How many bones does this guy have to break?

People drive by, their cars start to honk—
Look at that guy, he's riding a bronc!
The purpose of riding is to stay in the saddle.
To drive Bill to his senses, do we need a paddle?

Bill on his horse often looks quite nifty.
We hope he survives to the ripe age of fifty.
Let's donate some money and watch it all grow
And buy Bill a saddle made out of Velcro.

Reading a Poem

When reading a poem
do you cringe when seeing a word
that stops you in your tracks
and wonder what it means

Wouldn't it be more fun
to read a poem that doesn't require
a Rosetta Stone for comprehension

A pleasure it is to read a poem unclouded
with superfluous words
a verse that says come and sit
relax   enjoy the day   walk around a bit
dance a little   perhaps a waltz   perhaps a fox trot

a poem that elevates you
takes you to venues you have never been
enables you to revisit places
and emotions of your past
puts a smile on your face
and a tear in your eye

You may even take a nap if you wish
and dream of distant lands
of candlelit dinners
of the comely gal at the market
with flowing locks who smiles at you
as she bags your groceries

After your siesta
after your journey through the poem
you awake   refreshed.

August is ...

a poem in the *Trading Post,*
crafted by Ann of Summer Days.

We love the way she blends her words
and how she turns a phrase,

revealing for us the things
we often seem to neglect—

colors in the countryside,
flora we should recollect.

She brings us back to golden times
to ponder the gifts of Vermont.

A poem from Ann of Summer Days
is more than we could ever want.

for Ann B. Day, Vermont poet

Hair

Hair styles are changing every day,
I have a multiple choice
of what I want atop my head
to express my inner voice.
The options are quite extensive,
my brain will soon be hazy—
picking a style from this long list
will surely drive me crazy.

I could be hip and go dreadlocks
like snakes along my temple.
Or maybe corn rows would be cool,
creative, transcendental.
Or shave the sides and wax the top,
a Mohawk arched to the sky—
everyone's eyes will be on me
whenever I'm walking by.

Funky or shaggy, short or long,
not an easy decision.
Pony tail, flat top, blue or green—
what more can I envision?
With all the hair styles one can pick
inside this vast galaxy,
I think I'll just shave it all off
and go à la Agassi.

That Time of Year

It's that time of year when they are here
lurking behind every tree   every bush
peering in through your window at night
lying under your bed
screeching hellish sounds
that make your hair stand straight up

Don't say you don't know who they are
You absolutely know from the Scottish prayer
who they are
They are ghoulies   ghosties
long leggedy beasties
things that go bump in the night

I dare you to walk through the town's old cemetery
on a moonless night
Alone   by yourself
with the wind doing tricks
causing old oaks to creek
groan   whine
I dare you to walk it alone
They'll be there
behind antediluvian headstones
behind rugged bark maples
waiting for you

Your Edgar Allen Poevian tell-tale heart will
pound pound pound
like the drum drum drum
of a forlorn partridge
drumming for his mate

You'll try not to hear or see them
You'll try to focus on the straightest line
out of the cemetery
You'll pray more than you have ever prayed
Your eyes dare not look in the direction of
the ghoulish ghastly sounds
Oh god you cry
get me out of here
No more will you venture out on nights like this

Yes you know
You've always known
You know it's that time of year when they are here
lurking behind every tree   every bush
peering in through your window at night
lying under your bed
screeching hellish sounds
that makes your hair
stand straight up

I dare you to walk it on your own
on a moonless night through the haunted zone.

A Gallery on the Marsh

for Sue Westin and John Pitcher, Vermont artists

They paint at their studio   a gallery on the marsh
scenes from the natural world
animals walking   creatures hunting
birds in the air   on branches   on cliffs

Two artists
caress with their brushes
lay down gradients of color
of texture   of reality
bringing forth the inborn beauty   strength
wisdom   courage
of their chosen wildlife

Each cat   each eagle   each buffalo
each hawk
is at home on the paintings
They blend in within their environs

It's as if they flew down from the sky
jumped from the woods   from the prairie
onto the canvas
to finally find long life
and peace.

Tennis Player's Answering Machine

Sorry I can't return your serve
    so leave a message
    full of verve—
        forehand sweet
        and backhand thunder,
            volley now
            with name and number—
        and when I can
    it will be so fine
    to return your serve
down the line.

December 26

A million bucks
A cute brunette
A tennis racquet
A TV set

A maid to clean
A brand new truck
A Honda Hybrid
Where was that schmuck?

Brand new Carhartts
Warm new mittens
Lots of cat food
to give my kittens

My bills paid off
A home-cooked turkey
with all the fixin's
just for me

So that's my list
of everything
that Santa Claus
forgot to bring.

Nothing Is Impossible

Nulla è impossibile in the game of tennis
as the gritty Parisian red clay held
two athletic women in its coarse grip
and asked them to bring forth their gifts with a racquet.
A stoic Aussie and an extroverted Italian,
both agile athletes, thoroughbreds
in quest of the French Open title,
stood their ground and dug deep within.

It was quickness and defense against power and serve,
the panache of the Italian parrying the forehand of the Aussie.
Francesca and Samantha
brought forth their mettle and spirit
and played like champions
in pursuit of their first major title.

But when the final point was over,
when the clay dust had finally settled,
the winner of the Suzanne Lenglen Cup
was the gal who rolled on her back
and kissed the red clay.

And all of Italy knew that nulla è impossibile
in the game of tennis
as their Francesca stood there
soaking in the cheers of the crowd,
a smile stretching from ear to ear.

Glenn and the Bear

Glenn went hunting in the woods
early one Sunday morn.
It was not against his religion
so he took his bow along.
He saw some very fine deer
and one teensy-weensy hare,
Then from his tree-stand,
what did he see?
A great big Vermont black bear.

Glenn sat there wondering
what was on that big bear's mind.
Was he just rooting up apples
or did he want Glenn's large behind?
Should he try to shoot that bruin
or should he let him go?
Glenn's knees were shaking like Jell-O—
Should he voice a manly *hello*?

As the bear meandered closer
and munched apples from the ground,
Glenn raised an eye
to the Lord in the sky,
these words he did expound ...

"Oh Lord,
You delivered Daniel from the lion's den,
also, Jonah from the belly of a whale and then,
three Hebrew children from the fiery furnace,
as the Good Book did declare,
Oh lordy Lord, if you can't help me,
for goodness sake don't help that bear!"

Then the bear captured Glenn's scent
and changed its current plan,
his jowls were dripping saliva,
did he like the taste of man?
Glenn was filled with terror
and could not lift his bow,
so he raised his voice
to the Lord in the sky,
and shouted through his woe …

"Oh Lord, I have been the best dad,
and as for my wife, Charlene,
I sure have made her glad.
So if You help me this time,
I promise never more to sin,
and I'll stop drinking whiskey,
along with the beer and gin!"

Then the bear caught sight of Glenn
quivering there in the tree.
As the bear rose up on its hind legs,
Glenn had an uncontrolled pee.
The bear's drool ran profusely,
he let out a terrific growl.

Glenn wondered if it was time
to throw in the proverbial towel.

Glenn was crying and praying
as he felt the big bear's scoff.
Would he climb the tree and eat Glenn
or would he merely wander off?
That bear, he too was thinking—
should he snack on Glenn's big rump?
But he merely walked away,
right over the mountain's hump.

Glenn's knees soon stopped shaking
and he thanked the Lord on high,
he hustled down off that hemlock—
you should have seen him fly.
He sprinted down the trail
and reached his truck in haste.
He cranked and fired that engine
and sped off in a race.

No more will Glenn go hunting,
he'll merely stay at home,
where bears never come-a-calling,
and where they never roam.

"Glenn and the Bear" is loosely based on a hunting venture of the poet's friend, Glenn Anderson. The author wishes to thank George W. Fairman (1881-1962) and his 1903 song, "The Preacher and the Bear," for inspiration and a few choice refrains.

Collage de Fromage

I recently had the strong urge
to write a poem about cheese.
I decided to give it a shot,
but it may not be such a breeze.

I'd be glad to babble 'bout Brie
and possibly chatter on Cheddar.
I may render some Roquefort rantings
and fine tune my feelings on Feta.

I could even pick on Provolone,
say some sweet things of the Swiss,
and warn, that when eating Muenster,
you will want to refrain from the kiss.

I would never forget Mozzarella
and the God-given goodness of Gouda,
Some of these cheeses have survived
since the early days of the Buddha.

I won't stifle my citations of Stilton,
won't mumble on Monterey Jack,
I'll even pay tribute to Goat cheese,
and note Blue has nothing to lack.

I may even poke fun at Limburger
with its pungently alarming aroma.
Yet, many are those who love it—
they must all be in a coma.

Me, I can't live without Parmesan,
and love it atop my spaghetti—
I firmly grab hold of a grater
and find I'm producing confetti.

Yes, I'd be glad to put pen to paper
and attempt to chitchat on cheese,
but when it comes to these casein curds,
everyone eats what they please.

My Voice

for Travis Luxenberg and other individuals with autism

My words cut
through a silent world.
I hurl sounds
beyond the closet walls
that trap me.
I tread the treacherous sea of autism.
My words are my life preserver.

Delicate is my dance.
I shield myself
in my life's performance as only I know how.
My body and mind are sometimes
in rhythmic motion,
soothing me.

Few can understand,
can penetrate the peace within me.
At times my spirit thrives,
then walls close in,
the door slams shut.

Trapped inside,
I utter every word I can muster.
I am overpowered within these walls
of horrific confinement.
I am caged.

My oxygen is being exhausted.
Suffocation is inevitable
if I am not set free.
I beg! Open the door!
Please let me out of here!

I begin to see light
as my captors open the door.
A deathly hold has been broken.
My lungs breathe in the fresh air.
I exit with calmness
into a peaceful world,
content to be free.

My voice
must be heard.
No more
will the door be locked.

Written by Linda & Travis Luxenberg and Jerry Johnson. Linda was director
of Ellie's Place in Burlington, Vermont which provides social and recreational
programs for teens and young adults with autism.

If the Effort is There

Shall one strive and fall
or shall one strive and rise?
It makes no difference at all
if one really tries.

If the effort is there
with a goal out in front,
12.4 in the hundred
is still quite a stunt.

Yes, 12.4 in the hundred
and the mile under 9,
if the effort is there,
you're doing fine.

Written by the poet at the age of thirteen

Winged Victory

for Laura Lee Mount (6-years-old) and her stallion Taddas

Laura is atop her Arabian steed—
Taddas, grand Missisquoi stallion of white.
Winged horse and girl ride the wind,
Equine and rider—an incredible sight.

We stand and gaze, they're galloping our way,
And listen to thundering hoof-falls of Taddas.
With Laura at the reins, we have no concern
Though horse and rider are coming right at us.

The tinkling of bells on Taddas' breastplate
Contrasts to the rumbling of his hooves of might.
He carries his rider with the ease of a dancer,
On her face she emits a grin of delight.

There is something special about a girl and her horse—
A love and too many things to recount.
Rest assured that the stallion is in good hands,
Equestrian in charge—Laura Lee Mount.

The Taxman Cometh

for Francis Whitcomb

The lister called and left a message upon my machine,
"Jerry, it's Francis Whitcomb, not calling to be mean.
I see you've added to your barn a brand new addition.
See you tomorrow, hope it's not an imposition.
I will have to reassess the improvements at your farm.
Sorry to call on Sunday, I really wish no harm."

Next day, the assessor arrived promptly at 9 o'clock;
I greeted him after hearing that ominous knock.
"Good morning," said Sir Francis, "how are you this fine day?"
Said I, "Was better minutes ago, now skies are gray.
I see you have pen and paper and know why you have come—
to see my new addition, I'm starting to feel glum."

Now, Francis is a nice guy and quite pleasant in the main—
a cross twixt Abe Lincoln and Irving's Ichabod Crane.
I can't bear to see him coming to reappraise my home,
wish he would find a place on another street to roam.
He has a job to do and attempts to keep me at ease,
but I know when he's done, my wallet will feel the squeeze.

Some loathe going to the dentist, some fear doctors as well;
I dread the lister—it is enough to make me yell.
One can avoid the dentist, see the doc every five years,
but the lister is enough to bring grown men to tears.
So, if you get a call from this guy named Francis Whitcomb,
he'll be coming to visit—you'll be his next victim.

Hail to the Proletariat

Hail to those of the working division
who rise real early and work with precision,
men milking Holsteins down on their farms,
homemaking moms with babes in their arms.

Prayers to soldiers departing from home
to faraway places where they fear to roam,
leaving their fathers with crops in the fields,
farmers are hopeful for bountiful yields.

Praise to the kids selling daily news,
pedaling their bikes in worn-out shoes.
Kudos to loggers felling trees in the wood,
cutting timber for the common good.

Cheers to cops alone on their call
bringing a measure of protection for all;
to fearless firemen, lives in their care,
gnarly-handed cobblers with shoes to repair.

A toast to women and men on machines,
wearing plaid shirts and faded old jeans.
Here's to the postman delivering mail,
applause to the carpenter with hammer and nail.

A salute to the farrier, the sawyer, the fitter,
nary a one of them is ever the quitter.
So, hail to the people of backbreaking vocations,
pride of the land, fabric of the nation.

Lessons

At night I read a poem or two,
some Hayford, then some Frost,

my head upon a pillow,
my mind upon the cost

of what they had to do
to make their poems all rhyme.

As they tried to end each couplet,
did it click with them each time?

Kinnell, for him it's free verse,
no need for *tree* and *lee,*

he thinks the rhyme is dead
and the thought alone is key.

I mull over all of the greats,
each with their poetic bonanzas,

some stick to old-time rhymes,
others swear by free-form stanzas.

Creek Road Poet

The Creek Road Poet puts pen to the paper,
his words dance around as if on a caper.
He is only concerned if it will all blend
and he has no idea how it will end.

Reaching down deep the thoughts start to flow,
phrases come together like the kneading of dough.
And when it is finished he puts down the pen
and says to his poem, *Amen and Amen.*

The First Time

I was nineteen when we met
She was in her early twenties
It was my first time
I will always remember

Antoinette was her name
and it was summertime on the Cape
Our eyes first connected at a nightclub
She was a black-haired Italian beauty
with a dark easy-on-the-eyes radiant complexion
One never forgets these things

We danced   Later we drove
to a nearby beach and walked barefoot
in the sand   the tide coming in
waves gently fondling the shore
the light of a full moon laying
sparkles on the incoming tide

We walked   her hand in mine
I told stories   she smiled   laughed
then we paused and faced each other
eyes exchanging lingering gazes
I wondered what I would do   could do
should do   More than that
I wondered what she wanted

I wrapped my arms around her and felt
her warm body pressing against mine
She asked me to kiss her which I did
She asked again   this time a long slow kiss
The waves splashed against our feet
She said *Call me Toni*

In the fall we met again in Boston
Candles flickered throughout her apartment
We made love
My first time   not hers

Her skin was smooth and tight
her waist like a wasp
Her long black tresses cascaded over
her shoulders onto my face
She said *Kiss me*   Her lips were soft

We laid together   my arms around her
spooning together in a love knot
We fell asleep for a short while
but awoke to start again our
slow pulsating love making
love making into the night
It was my first time
I will always remember.

Chapter 4

Time and Place

Horse dance under a Vermont moon painted on antique sap bucket cover

The Farm Along the Creek

When his father passed away
he inherited the farm along the creek.
His dad knew it was where his son's heart was,
where it always had been from the beginning.

The son loved discovering nature,
living close to the earth,
playing and fishing in the creek, camping,
hiking the hills and meadows of the farm.

The farm was alive with history,
a century of comings and goings,
a certain vibrancy of life,
a certain wildness.

Its new owner would see to it
that the farm would maintain
its bucolic footprint on the earth, as he dove
right in and brought more life, more soul.

Horses, dogs and barn cats found a home
at the farm. The son would cut and bale hay,
maintain fences, renovate the old farmhouse
and restore the old barn.

His mind became full with memories
of swimming in the creek,
catching brookies in the pond,
sleeping in the sugarhouse,

memories of relatives
who used to visit in days gone by,
but whose lives got caught up
with other things.

Then there were more memories
shared with old and new friends
who came to join in life's happenings,
nature's constant change.

Fond recollections of riding his horse,
walking his dogs, and making hay
in the warm summer sun
filled his thoughts.

Content is he, as are his animals.
Each day is a new day. Each day
something new is discovered.
Each dawn brings them a new awakening.

Whenever I see a Turtle

for Mary Oliver

Whenever I see a turtle
I'm reminded to slow down.
What's the rush? True friends will wait,
will understand, will help.
Miss. Harris, my junior high math teacher,
frequently said to the class (or was it just to me?):
Patience is a virtue.
It's funny how you remember things like that,
several decades later.
Turtles are assuredly patient. They like
sitting on a rock as they soak in the noonday sun.
You never see them sprinting across a street.
Perhaps they are hopeful that a good Samaritan
will give them a helping hand
and bring them to safety.
I say, *Forget the eye of the tiger.* We should pay
closer attention to the eye of the turtle.

Stone and Wood

for my father

Out walking on a moonlit eve
deep within the woods,
I came across a wall of stone.
Nearly three foot high it rose,
a woven rope of rock trailing beneath bending trees.

A canopy of leaves sifted moonbeams
dancing light on old stones,
and lichen like lace
lay over boulders in the secluded wall.

A flat rock invited me to sit.
I let my eyes contemplate
the stillness of this scene,
my mind works back—
this must have been a farmer's wall
one hundred years ago.

I see his thick hands clearing trees—
pasture for his cows.
And with a horse-drawn plow he turns the ground,
freeing countless stones from their earthen graves.
The woods removed and soil plowed twice,
young backs and hands strain to raise stones.

The sun bakes down,
sweat pours freely, hands blister and bleed.
Work continues day after day—
sons and daughters of the farmer
are picking stones, picking stones,
picking stones.

Along a chosen route
they position each rock and boulder,
some small, some monolithic,
all placed in perfect stasis,
wedged well on the promise of those below.

Four feet high the bulwark grows,
a half-mile or more uncoiling,
an ever-growing divider
snaking along the uneven forest floor.

One hundred years of heaving frosts
toppled sections of the ancient wall.
The once-level crown undulates,
yet the elongated cairn still stands,
marking its place in the woods.

The forest has returned,
as it was before the farmer came—
fir and beech, cedar and maple,
here and there a tamarack.

Near the wall of stone lies the rusted skeleton
of the farmer's Model T,
firmly anchored to the ground by a massive oak,
growing true from the innards
of the corroded horseless carriage.

The wall has not changed much
in the passing decades;
the woods has reclaimed its primordial home
where the pasture once lay.
These odd neighbors remain themselves.
One stands at rest, the other never stops—
this mutually acceptable
coexistence of stone and wood.

They still tell their story.
The ever-changing woodland
doesn't mind the stark reality of the wall
that stands as a monument
to the farmer and his cows.

I sit, quiet,
listen to the stories offered.
Perhaps, in time, their meaning will surface.
But for now this flat rock,
that young maple,
and the rugged oak have much to tell,
and I am in no hurry.

Home

Now as the sun sets over green mountains
closing a perfect day in Vermont
I stare into the night sky
and contemplate the peacefulness
of this bucolic setting
and wonder if it will last

I smell teddered hay in the hayfield
as it slowly cures
readying itself for tomorrow's baling
I listen to water in the stream rushing along
as it rolls over boulder and rock
I watch a night owl whisper his way above quiet trees
as he seeks a resting spot on the limb of a maple
I take notice of a chorus of coyotes
crying out in the distance
as they begin their evening search for food

I hear a killdeer's cacophony as her
penetrating *kill-dee   kill-dee   dee-dee-dee*
fills the valley floor
My horses mosey to the
far corner of the pasture down by the creek
I follow them
Their bodies are soon silhouetted
by the light of a full moon
They look my way and whinny
then begin to graze
Such peace and harmony
such contentment here in the north country
I hope it lasts.

He's Not Calling Anymore

He's not calling anymore
And sharing dreams as done before.
She was his woman, but she done him wrong,
And muted the music of his song.

He thought that she would've listened to
All his words, his I-love-you.
She left without a parting word,
'twas only silence that he heard.

No rocks to skip across the lake,
No wishing wells, no give and take.
No more to vie on right and wrong,
No poem to read, no voice in song.

> He's not calling anymore
> And sharing dreams as done before.
> She was his woman, but she done him wrong,
> And muted the music of his song.

Time has passed and they have parted,
And left a world for the broken-hearted.
No hand-in-hand, no more to share,
Mum is the music of their love affair.

He's not calling anymore
And sharing dreams as done before.
She was his woman, but she done him wrong,
And muted the music of his song.

But he will rise and sing again
And find himself another friend.
He'll share his dreams, walk hand-in-hand
With a woman who will understand.

In harmony they'll dance along
With a poem in rhyme and a voice in song.
New rocks to skip across that lake
New wishing wells and give and take.

Together they'll join and sing again
Words and song in perfect blend.
Countless brand-new dreams to share,
Alive in the music of their love affair.

The Barn

Old barn
rustic structure of beam and peg
framed with love in days of yore

you stand today on wobbly posts
and members weak from age

It's time to go
your job complete
the roof protects you not

The leaning of your body
brings tears to passers by
Some groan
some wonder why

The barn groans back
and does its best
to pose in grandeur long forgotten

Perhaps the barn
is saying that all things pass us by

and journeys that
the journeyman takes
must have a finish line

So before you fall
we will take you down
one section at a time

save some timbers
straight and true
and build a new barn

Phoenix-like it will stand within
your old footprint
and help fill the emptiness

of the vacant spot

and the emptiness
we will feel when you are gone.

A Walk on a Country Road

I will take a walk today down an old country road
My pace will be slow as I want to take in each blossom
on a gnarly apple tree next to the stonewall
which meanders along the road

I will sit at times on the wall
and smell the newly mown hay
I will watch bluebirds and swallows
drifting on warm currents of air

I will gaze at a soaring hawk
as he   with binocular eyes
takes in everything he pinpoints below
What a sight that will be

I will listen for sounds of natural things
water cascading down a mountain stream

the thunderous tail whack of a dam builder
dissonant reverberations of spring peepers
shrill cries of a killdeer protecting her young

ratta-tat-tats of a pileated pirate jackhammering a dead elm
and the soothing chicka-dee-dee-dee of a black-capped songster

I will walk at a slow pace   listen to thoughts coming in
later put them into words of the places I have been
I will recall the crooning of doves   aroma of hay in the field
Contented my soul will be   having observed nature's yield.

The Sun Sets Early

The sun sets early this time of year—
it's all part of the scheme of things.
During the summer
the sun drenches our souls
with enduring warmth ...

hopefully with enough internal heat
to take us from November
to April.

School Bell

Each morning at 8 a.m. you would
ring out to the countryside,
casting a spell on those within earshot
as you sold education with your song.
Students were called to come and learn.

You pealed loud and clear
across the valley and to the hills beyond,
so that kids, even those a mile away,
would hear you and knew it was time
to start their morning walk
to join forces with their friends
in the one-room schoolhouse.

A young teacher greeted each child
with a big *Good morning*
and each child would reply with
Good morning, Miss. Villeneuve.

Children of all ages, grades 1 through 6,
dressed in clean blouses and skirts,
knickers and laced-up shoes
sat at their desks,
ready to be challenged, ready to learn.

The morning passed by quickly
and at noon it was time for recess.
Children rushed from their desks
and headed outside.
Some ran to the swings and seesaws,
others to the field out back,
some to the creek
to see if they could catch a frog.

Soon you would ring out your song again
and call the students to come and learn.
They would rush from the swings and seesaws,
from the field, from the creek,
and quickly find their seats
and prepare themselves for their next lesson.

At 3:00 p.m. the school day was over
and children began walking
back home to their farmhouses.
Little Joey didn't walk.
He ran as fast as he could
since he could hardly wait to show his mom
the big bullfrog he had in his pocket.

On the Day of Her Birth

Little girl Quinn has arrived
to bless a family and home
on Town Farm Road
A package of tender beauty is she
all dependency and love
so small yet so strong

A bond will blossom
as doting members of Quinn's kin
gather 'round her 24/7
to love and protect her
to teach her the ways
of worldly wise

Little girl Quinn has arrived
to bring a smile to an uncle faraway
dressed in coveralls
feeding his horses
by the light of a full moon
cascading over meadow
and distant hills

And in the late evening
in the silence of his study
his golden at his feet
he will attempt to write a poem
about the truth
beauty and innocence
of a little one.

Haying is Such Sweet Sorrow

Scene 1:

Ah, haying is such sweet sorrow,
will I start my haying tomorrow?
I must start my haying soon,
either by day or the light of the moon.

I pray for sunny days ahead,
no more rain which I dread.
To make those sweet bales of hay,
all wet weather must stay away.

Scene 2:

Yesterday the sun showed bright,
and not a cloud was within eyesight.
I attached the mower to the John Deere,
headed to the hayfield full of cheer,

and mowed in circles going clockwise
ten acres of meadow under pleasant skies.
At eight in the eve my job was done,
gave my thanks to the setting sun.

At ten the weather began to change,
thunder and lightning were within close range.
The heavens opened with a huge downpour,
my dogs were scared, I merely swore.

What's with rain on my new mown hay!
Couldn't it wait for another day?
Will tomorrow's sun shine like today?
You need good weather when you hay.

Scene 3:

Today was a blessing for the job at hand,
sun was glowing, life was grand.
I headed out with my tractor
and knew that rain wouldn't be a factor.

I teddered the hay to help it dry,
it's easy to do with sun in the sky.
I pray that tomorrow will be like today,
so I can bale that sweet mown hay!

Scene 4:

Alas, six-hundred bales scattered in the field—
the lovely bounty of nature's yield.
Into the barn they'll find their way.
Nothing's easy, making hay.

Warm Greetings

Warm Green Mountain greetings from my old farm
No creature stirring   the horses are calm
Birdfeeders provide for sparrow and dove
Blue jays and finches all send you their love

Fresh deer tracks encircle the wild apple trees
Where were they in Autumn   they're such a tease
On the pond thick with ice kids skate with great glee
I keep the snow cleared with my trusty ATV

While snowshoeing right by the old sugar shack
What do I spy but another deer track
Cross-country skiing o'er meadows and hills
A north country winter has wonderful thrills.

Campfire Song

The twigs in the campfire
the leaves in the campfire
make the fire grow

The sticks in the campfire
the logs in the campfire
make the fire glow

The mountains so high
up against the sky
look down on us below

as we sit around the campfire
and sing songs
which we all know

Coyotes wail their song to the moon
an owl hoots for his mate
trout rise for flies on the pond
and the hour is getting late

We join with the chorus of coyotes
with the owl we hoot right along
a chorale of man and critter
together in a song

The sticks and logs are dying out
darkness replaces light
It's time for us to lay down our heads
time to say goodnight.

A Girl with a Curl

As she was being pushed along
in her comfy stroller by her loving nana,
she smiled at me. I smiled back
and all the pressures of the day,
all the things on my to-do list
became secondary to that precious happy smile
on her precious happy face.

Her big sky-blue eyes glistened—
sparkling indigo orbs
which did not miss a trick
and stared straight into mine.
Perhaps she was wondering
who this tall guy was,
this guy dressed in coveralls
and a baseball cap.

Perhaps she was thinking
Don't you just love this
beautiful Vermont day?
Don't you want to know my name?

Her naturally curly hair
was her crowning tiara.
She must be the Queen of the Kingdom.
One curl zigzagged delicately down her forehead.

My goodness, is your name Shirley Temple?
What a pretty smile you have. What pretty blue eyes.
What beautiful curly brown hair.
Do you want to dance?
You can be Shirley Temple,
I'll be Mr. Bojangles.

Her nana said *Jerry, this is Isabella.*
She is twenty months old.
Isabella, this is Jerry.

A big grin stretched on my face.
Isabella, it's nice to meet you.
What a pretty name you have.
I love your smile. I hope we meet again.
Goodbye, my new friend.

My serendipitous meeting with Isabella
on a clear summer day in Vermont
was a wonderful reminder to be on the lookout
for unexpected treasures
appearing in small packages ...

One never knows when
a girl with a curl
may plant a smile on your face
free of charge.

Monstrous Gluk and Gobbledygook

Monstrous gluk and gobbledygook
    And felonious times at the fair
Mischievous monks and elephant trunks
    And castles in clouds by the square

Millicent micks and dogs doing tricks
    Flowers with petals aflutter
Birds in the sky that never know why
    And flies that land in my butter

Opocuring my car to an alleyway bar
    One wheel not following the other
The sun going down at the end of the town
    And I'm late for dinner with mother

Flambonious mud to my friend named Bud
    Dressed in his white suit with tails
He dances with bears between all the chairs
    And falls in a bucket of nails

Sangrecious sangria after losing Lucia
    Will ease all the pain in the storm
Repertentious reptilians look like Sicilians
    Coming out like bees in a swarm

Capacorio clamor as the bell meets the hammer
  Melancopolous misfits abound
Silly centurions eating like epicureans
  Consume everything that is found

Monstrous gluk and gobbledygook
  And felonious times at the fair
Mischievous monks and elephant trunks
  And castles in clouds by the square.

Too Many

Stop the war, cease and desist,
when attempting to kill, try to resist.

Enough have fallen,
one more is too many—
too many dads and too many sons,
too many daughters,
too many, too many.

Tears have fallen,
too many tears,
hearts have been broken
for too many years.

Brothers are gone, sisters are gone,
never to return,
too many, too many.

Too much insanity,
too much, too much,
too little sanity,
too little, too little.

Lost is a son, lost is a daughter,
too little love, too much slaughter.
Enough have fallen, when will it be stopped?
Too many have passed, too many have dropped.

Too many gravestones,
too many flowers,
too many have passed
from these homes of ours.

Tim Barry is an artist. I own a number of his paintings. We are friends, yet we have never met. Tim has been in prison for about 30 years. I purchased his paintings from his sister, Mary Lou, who sells his artwork. After I acquired a couple of his paintings, I wrote him a letter. Although he is incarcerated, he is permitted to receive and send letters. He is not allowed to receive calls or e-mails from the outside world. He then sent a letter to me. This is what started our friendship. We have communicated several times by letter. I told him how much I love his artwork. I also sent him poems. His letters revealed to me what an incredible person he is. His letters showed me what made him tick, what kept him going in spite of his confinement behind bars. Our communication resulted in the following poem.

A Communiqué

The poet writes to the artist   caged behind bars
serving 30 years as punishment for what the poet surmises
must have resulted from a brief moment of anger ...

    Your beautiful paintings hang on my farmhouse walls
    They brighten each room and bring joy to all who see them
    How can an artist paint such exquisite scenes
    from within confined quarters?

The artist ...

    Art has become my life and salvation
    However   at night
    when it is quiet here
    I hear truck tires singing on the pavement on I-93
    and I get a hankering to feel wheels
    rolling under me   crossing the continent
    running the flats   pulling the mountains

Sometimes I can still hear the tone
of the engine surge after a downshift on a hard pull
This has become a long hard pull for me
but I have paint   and it doesn't matter
to an artist if a sunrise is viewed
from a palace or a prison
The light and colors
are the same

The poet ...

You are a skilled artist
Your paintings reflect beauty and truth
and the healing of a resurrected man
a man who has paid his dues
and should now be set free
You are also adept at writing what you feel
Your words are poetic

The artist ...

I will leave the language to you poets
I've come to be skeptical of words
in the hands of politicians   authoritarians   and lawyers
I'm in the past with Voltaire   Emerson
and the Zen writings of Dōgen
There is still beauty in those words
I make sure to read T. S. Elliot's Four Quartets
at least once a year
I lean toward the mystical side of life

The poet sends some of his poems to the artist one of which includes . . .

> Beneath a bed of leaves
> all things are made afresh
> as babes without a blemish
> ascending to the sun
> to start once more with shackles gone
> to stretch and touch their dreams
> A new beginning comes with forgiveness and rebirth
> rooted deep and pressing out
> beneath a bed of leaves

The artist . . .

> Your poems have put me in the Kingdom for a while
> Thank you for the crunch of the snow
> the smell of the woods   the spirits of animals
> A Bed of Leaves is my favorite
> Try to put your mind in prison
> and read it slowly
> It is a Zen-mind-like
> salvific message   ". . . to start once more with shackles gone"
> Great stuff

The poet . . .

> You should be released
> Your debt has been paid
> in time   in paint
> in words

The artist ...

> I've carried an idea for a long time
> When I get out I want to go to an animal shelter
> find the meanest dog of the lot
> and give it a home
> A dog that no one else wants
> that's the dog I want
> even if I have to talk nicely and feed it dog biscuits
> every day for a month to gain its trust
> That dog and I would understand each other

The poet sends photos of the artist's paintings to his confined friend ...

> Your letter was quite moving and poetic
> I hope we can continue to communicate
> All four of your works hang handsomely in my farmhouse
> Here are some pics

The artist ...

> Thanks so much for the photos of my artwork
> hanging on your walls
> I usually don't know where they go
> or what they look like framed up
> Many of my paintings stem from
> my imagination and memory
> others are from photos people send
>
> I've recently ventured into some abstract painting
> and like the freedom of using color for effect
> It's different   but I don't expect that I'll
> venture far from representational realism
> I'm really attached to the Zen Buddhist ideal
> and meditate a lot

The abstract expressionist scheme is good
for rendering ideas such as
peace within chaos or impermanence
I have a nice photo of Mount Mansfield I want to work with
and a couple of close up shots of a snowy owl
I think the owl will need a fence post and a lot of snow

The artist ...

People are usually curious about what prison is like
It's long periods of boredom   interspaced with
short periods of intense excitement   fear when
things get stupid
Prison is like having your entire life ordered
by the bureaucrats at the vehicle registry
For the most part it exacerbates existing problems
and further alienates the marginal
What I've come to know is that ignorance
is the enemy of all that is worthwhile
and if the world is destroyed
it will be militant ignorance that does it in
Please take care

The poet …

I sit here
typing away at a poem
which reflects the writings and musings
of me and my new friend
I am free   liberated
as I observe the natural world around me
ready at a whim to write a poem about bluebirds
nesting in a nearby birdhouse
I am without shackles to curb
the words I want to write

My friend sits behind bars of steel
Yet he finds beauty from within
and is able to brush it onto canvases
to produce works of splendor

He brings hope to himself
and to those who have one of his creations
hanging in a place of honor

My home is blessed to have the artist's paintings
adorning its walls
and I am blessed to have the artist as my friend.

Coming into Middle Age

Coming into middle age,
I thought I'd wake to be a sage.
Wisdom would clearly flow from me
and ears would turn toward my decree.
Childish eyes would surely see
my cognitive insight, aujourd'hui.

Children are the ones to scout,
they know what life is all about—
at play within their world of dreams,
chasing windmills, making schemes,
alive in the moment, no lists to make,
just having fun, for goodness' sake.

So, if in aging I seek to exist
among the gurus, I must resist
temptations of a cluttered mind.
While watching children I will find
total freedom and fearless deeds—
heroic kids, planting seeds.

To Where Does Time Fly?

Where does time fly to when it wants to fly?
Does it retreat to a daisy or rose?
Does it hide from the warmth of midday sun?
Does it drift in a river? Who knows?

Is time the main factor to getting old
as we venture through life every day?
Does the clock keep cadence to our course?
Does time ever stand still? Who can say?

Some people choose to live in the future
while others are bogged down in the past.
I try to dwell on things as they happen,
knowing time marches on much too fast.

On the Passing of My Beloved Barn Cat

Because I will outlive you
should I tell you to love me less
so my grief at your departing lessens?

The lessons of life are simple
We live a life and die
leaving our mark on hearts that beat
on minds that lean on stuff stiffer
than flesh with fur or skin
or eyes that shine in the dark
Don't despair
Life is fair
We are all under the same aegis

Pinkie … I have outlived you …
you should have died hereafter …
perhaps there would have been a time for such a word

But your brief time here was such a grand one …
I cherished every day
which began with your greeting me at the door
as I headed out to the barn
a huge container of cat food in hand
to feed you and your brother and sister
all three hairy bundles of energy
leading the way
tails raised straight up like periscopes
each of you taking turns
rolling in the grass

As I proceeded to unlock the barn door
Pinkie … Blackie … then Lady Gray
would zigzag around the cuffs
of my coveralls and purr their blessed purr
It was their daily morning ritual
and I was a willing happy participant

Each of you celebrated other rites throughout the day …
hanging out with the horses in the barn
weaving your ways from one stall to another
catnapping high up on the bales of hay in the loft
catching mice (are there any left?)
sneaking up on birds (hope you didn't catch any)
drinking from the horses' tall water trough (quite the balancing act)

But my favorite tradition
came in the early evening during twilight time …
I would sit on the stoop of the back porch
and call your names

Each of you would push against the loose weathered board
on the barn door
and squeeze your way out …
You came sauntering up to me
and each of you would say
Pick me up … make my motor hum

And yes Pinkie
your motor did hum.

Harvest Moon

It's October at the farm—
a transitional month between
fall and winter.
The Harvest Moon has signaled
the end of the growing season,
the beginning of early morning frosts
and gossamer-iced ponds,
crackling fires in the woodstove.

The farmer has geared up
for a winter fast approaching.
He wonders what will come
as do his horses who stand and stare,
waiting for a treat from
the man in his coveralls.

He always brings treats ...
they hope for apples
today.

Early Morning

Early morning at the farm
Coffee brewing
Poet at his desk   writing
Fire crackling in the woodstove
Sundance absorbing radiating warmth
Toby waiting for a cookie

Summer whispered away long ago
Changes in the air
Autumn leaves tumbling
Rain gently beating on the roof
Fall disappearing bit by bit
Chickadees assailing the birdfeeder
Winter slowly sneaking in
Early morning at the farm.

Christmas Eve

The farm is asleep on Christmas Eve
Three mares and a gelding stand as statues
in a snow-covered pasture
their nostrils steaming the icy air

Two barn cats slumber
curled up on bales of sweet hay
The old barn creaks
in rhythm with a pulsating north wind

Four deer weave through a cedar swamp
finding their way to a field along Lord's Creek
They nibble on grasses still not totally buried
'neath a white blanket

It is peaceful in the valley at the farm
The caretaker lies at rest on a brass bed
One golden dozes beside him
the other at the foot of his bed

He will arise at five
don his coveralls
boots and mittens
head out to greet his horses and cats
and give them Christmas breakfast.

On nights like this ...

I think about her
as I sit in the dark
my golden retriever lying at my feet
Candles flicker on the fireplace mantle
The wind blows gently outside
during this warm Vermont evening

My thoughts are on a gentle being
who touches me
her stroke that of an angel

Such good fortune do I have in her company
A certain warmth and gentleness
emanates from her aura   is exposed in her smile
I am in the presence of a friend and lover
an understanding woman
who makes me feel at ease

Her life is lived in placid terms
a legacy of truth and inner beauty
of balance and trust

On nights like this when I am alone
I think of my beauty   my lover
for she is here   a peaceful spirit
rejoicing in my thoughts

Lying in bed I again ponder
Might she be thinking about me?
Would she like to be held close?
Would she like warm hugs?
Would she like tender kisses?
Does she want me making love to her?

I hope we are on the same page
with similar vibrations   similar excitement
similar dreams

A smile comes to my face
a certain contentment as I fall asleep
and dream about her
my beauty   my lover   my friend.

Pondering

A cool evening mist tiptoed across the valley
causing us to ponder the approaching fall
when leaves will turn.
We hope that their changeover will be one only of color,
not a turning against us,
not a foreboding omen of things to come.

Is summer winding down much too quickly yet again?
It always seems that summers come with barely a whisper
and depart with hardly a warning.

Will we be geared up for winter?
Winters which sneak in with a few flurries,
a thin mantle of ice upon the pond.
They break us in slowly
but surely.

And come December
when we gather around warm stoves,
we will again ponder ...
this time about the summer to come
so many months away.

A Certain Ebb

It is November here at the farm.
Some may say that November is
neither an autumn month
nor a winter month.
Perhaps it is the twilight zone of
months in the north country.
Some may say it is a month
where beauty has departed. I think not.

I love the russet colors of pastures
and hayfields, trees without leaves—
skeletons with many arms
lifted skyward,
crunchy echoes of footfalls on frozen leaves,
first ice on the pond,
first dusting of snow,
one's breath vaporizing into the cool air,
sound of wood crackling
in the old Crawford cookstove,
aroma of hot cross buns in the oven,
the strong morning sun
casting an early glow over the meadow.

There is a certain ebb to the seasons
when November arrives.
Autumn colors have waned,
mornings begin with window frost,
geese have departed
and winter is lurking behind the hills.

The wood has been stacked, shutters are on,
the to-do list has been chipped away ...
this time of year
I'm usually in recuperatio modus.

It is also a time for contemplation,
for renewal, for reprieve,
a time to look outward and inward
and to discover, once again,
the beauty without and within—
the beauty of one's surroundings ...

all in preparation for things
to come—
a thick and white winter just ahead.

Break Clear Away

"Keep close to Nature's heart ... and break clear away, once in awhile, and climb a mountain or spend a week in the woods. Wash your spirit clean."

—John Muir

Let's break clear away together
just you and me
We'll find a secret hiding place
'neath a big old tree

Let's venture down a woodland path
blaze a brand new trail
and find the place where coyotes sing
as do the hawk and quail

Let's go where others dare not pass
We'll climb a hill and yell
Let our echoes resonate
through mountaintop and dell

Find a pond and jump right in
purify body and soul
With no one there to watch us
who cares if we lose control

Let's breathe afresh the mountain air
cool through every pore
dance along with Pan and Faun
upon a pine needled floor

And discover what we're seeking
it's right there 'round those bends
We'll uncover the answer on our quest
and find we are best friends.

About the Author

Jerry Johnson taught at Fitchburg State University in Massachusetts where he was a finalist for the Dr. Vincent J. Mara Award for Excellence in College Teaching. Jerry lives on a bucolic farm in Vermont's verdant Northeast Kingdom. The stimulus for much of his work stems from the natural beauty of this Vermont locale.

Several of the author's poems and stories have appeared in Vermont publications, including *The Mountain Troubadour, the Chronicle, North Star Monthly, Green Mountain Trading Post, Caledonian Record, Hardwick Gazette, Newport Daily Express* and *Vermont's Northland Journal*.

Since 2001, Jerry has been a contributor (tennis poems and stories) to the *New England Senior Tennis Foundation Bulletin,* which reaches thousands of readers throughout New England and the U.S. His poetry has appeared in *Tennis Week* magazine. He has been a freelance writer for the *Worcester (MA) Telegram & Gazette.*

Jerry is an active member of the League of Vermont Writers, Poetry Society of Vermont, Burlington Writers Workshop and Poetry Society of New Hampshire. The Poetry Society of Vermont presented him the Corrine Eastman Davis Memorial Award for his poem "Sugaring." His poem "Tennis Player's Answering Machine" was a winner in the Second Annual Poetry Challenge, sponsored by Wonderland Books of Putnam, Connecticut.

Jerry is a graduate of the University of Massachusetts in Amherst where he was bestowed with the Eastern College Athletic Conference Award as the school's top scholar-athlete. He has been ranked in the top 10 in New England tennis and has captured numerous championships.

Up the Creek Without a Saddle is Jerry's second book of poetry. His first, *A Bed of Leaves*, was published in 2004.

Made in the USA
Charleston, SC
03 November 2016